Discover Sharks

TIGER SHARK

Camilla de la Bédoyère

QED Publishing

Copyright © QED Publishing 2012

First published in the UK in 2012 by
QED Publishing
A Quarto Group company
230 City Road
London EC1V 2TT

www.qed-publishing.co.uk

A catalogue record for this book is available from
the British Library.

ISBN 978 1 78171 067 8

Printed in China

Consultant Mary Lindeed
Editor Tasha Percy
Designer Melissa Alaverdy

Picture credits
Key: t = top, b = bottom,
m = middle, l = left, r = right

Alamy Geoffrey Kidd 12b, Andre Seale 20-21
Dreamstime Idreamphotos 16-17
Getty Images Visuals Unlimited, Inc./Andy Murch 1
OceanwideImages.com 18-19
Photoshot Franco Banfi/Ocean Image 19r
Seapics.com 4-5, 5b, 6-7, 12-13, 14-15, 16b, 22-23
Shutterstock irabel8 2-3, A Cotton Photo 7t, 10-11, 24,
FAUP 8-9, Irina Moskalev 17t

Words in **bold** are explained in the Glossary on page 24

CONTENTS

WHAT IS A TIGER SHARK?

A tiger **shark** is a big **fish**.

Tiger sharks have
stripes like tigers do.
Some tiger sharks have
spots instead
of stripes.

stripes

spots

OCEAN LIFE

Tiger sharks live in warm oceans. They live near the shore. They can find food to eat there.

Tiger sharks swim in deep water in the daytime.

They swim in shallow water at night.

7

LIVING IN WATER

Sharks use **gills** to breathe in water.

gills

fin

They use **fins** to help them swim.

EYES AND NOSE

Look at the
shark's head.
It has big eyes.
It has a nose.

A shark's nose is called a **snout**.

eye

Tiger sharks can see and smell other animals in the water. They can taste and hear them in the water too.

11

SHARK TEETH

A shark has lots of teeth! How many teeth are in this shark's mouth? How many teeth do you have?

This is a tiger shark's tooth. It is very sharp.

Real size!

tooth

STRONG SWIMMER

Tiger sharks are strong swimmers. They swim slowly when they are looking for food.

This tiger shark sees something it wants to eat. Now it will swim very fast!

ATTACK!

A shark moves fast when it attacks an animal. It grabs the animal in its big mouth.

fish

seal

sea turtle

Tiger sharks hunt fish, baby sharks and **seals**. They also eat sea snakes, sea turtles and sea birds.

BINS WITH FINS

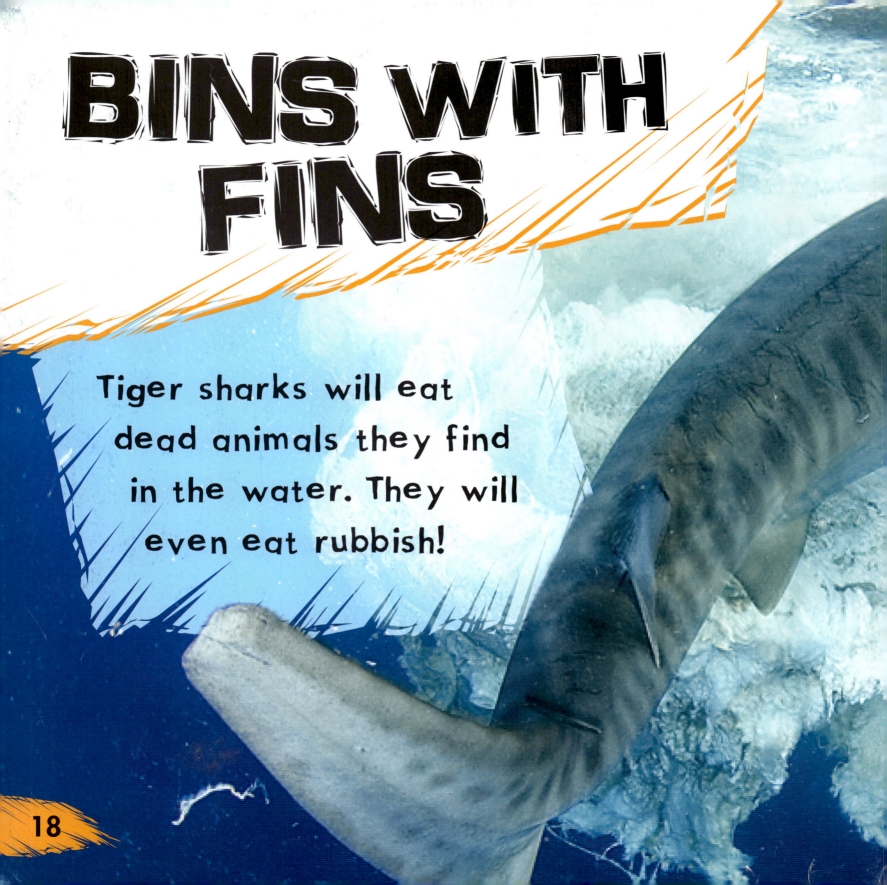

Tiger sharks will eat dead animals they find in the water. They will even eat rubbish!

dead whale

dead fish

Tiger sharks are sometimes called "bins with fins".

TIGER PUPS

Tiger sharks have babies in the spring or summer. A baby shark is called a **pup**.

A group of pups is called a litter. A mother shark can have 80 pups in just one litter.

pup

Now we know that tiger sharks are amazing animals!

22

GLOSSARY

fin   a part on the body of a fish shaped like a flap, used for moving and steering through the water

fish   a cold-blooded animal that lives in water and has scales, fins and gills

gill   the part of the body on a fish's side through which it breathes

pup   a young shark

seal   a sea mammal that lives in coastal waters and has thick fur and flippers

shark   a large and often fierce fish that feeds on meat and has very sharp teeth

snout   the long front part of an animals' head, including the nose, mouth and jaws